**BEARCUB BIOS**



# ZENDAYA

## ACTOR AND SINGER

by Rachel Rose

Consultant: Beth Gambro
Reading Specialist, Yorkville, Illinois

BEARPORT PUBLISHING

Minneapolis, Minnesota

# Teaching Tips

## BEFORE READING

- Discuss what a biography is. What kinds of things might a biography tell a reader?
- Look through the glossary together. Read and discuss the words.
- Go on a picture walk, looking through the pictures to discuss vocabulary and make predictions about the text.

## DURING READING

- Encourage readers to point to each word as it is read. Stop occasionally to ask readers to point to a specific word in the text.
- If a reader encounters an unknown word, ask them to look at the rest of the page. Are there any clues to help them understand?

## AFTER READING

- Check for understanding.
  - Where did Zendaya grow up?
  - What does she do?
  - What does she care about?
- Ask the readers to think deeper.
  - If you met Zendaya, what question would you like to ask her? Why?

**Credits:**
Cover and title page, © Jstone/Shutterstock and © Andrea Raffin/Shutterstock; 3, © Gregg DeGuire/Getty Images; 5, © UPI/Alamy Stock Photo; 7, © Bill McCay/Getty Images; 9, © Valerie Macon/Getty Images; 10-11, © Josiah Kamau/Getty Images; 12T, © Gregg DeGuire/Getty Images; 12B, © Gregg DeGuire/Getty Images; 13, © Bob D'Amico/Getty Images; 14-15, © Adam Taylor/Getty Images; 16-17, © Jennifer Lourie/Contributor/Getty Images; 18-19, © Kimberly White/Getty Images; 21, © Dfree/Shutterstock; 22, © Jaguar PS/Shutterstock; 23TL, © Andrey Danilovich/iStock; 23TR, © Deagreez/iStock; 23BL, © Dragon Images/Shutterstock; and 23BR, © SnvvSnvvSnvv/Shutterstock.

*Library of Congress Cataloging-in-Publication Data*

Names: Rose, Rachel, 1968– author. Title: Zendaya : actor and singer / by Rachel Rose. Description: Minneapolis, Minnesota : Bearport Publishing, [2021] | Series: Bearcub bios | Includes bibliographical references and index. Identifiers: LCCN 2020003672 (print) | LCCN 2020003673 (ebook) | ISBN 9781642809855 (library binding) | ISBN 9781642809961 (paperback) | ISBN 9781647470074 (ebook) Subjects: LCSH: Zendaya, 1996– —Juvenile literature. | African American motion picture actors and actresses—United States—Biography—Juvenile literature. | Motion picture actors and actresses—United States—Biography—Juvenile literature. | Television actors and actresses—United States—Biography—Juvenile literature. | African American women—Biography—Juvenile literature. Classification: LCC PN2287.Z47 R67 2021 (print) | LCC PN2287.Z47 (ebook) | DDC 791.4302/8092 [B]—dc23 LC record available at https://lccn.loc.gov/2020003672 LC ebook record available at https://lccn.loc.gov/2020003673



For more information, write to Bearport Publishing, 5357 Penn Avenue South, Minneapolis, MN 55419.

# Contents


**Movie Star of the Year . . . . . . . . . . 4**

**Zendaya's Life . . . . . . . . . . . . . . . . . . 6**

Did You Know? . . . . . . . . . . . . . . . . . . . . . . . . . . . . 22

Glossary . . . . . . . . . . . . . . . . . . . . . . . . . . . . . . . 23

Index . . . . . . . . . . . . . . . . . . . . . . . . . . . . . . . . . 24

Read More . . . . . . . . . . . . . . . . . . . . . . . . . . . . . 24

Learn More Online . . . . . . . . . . . . . . . . . . . . . . . 24

About the Author . . . . . . . . . . . . . . . . . . . . . . . . 24

# Movie Star of the Year

Zendaya smiled at the crowd.

She was very happy.

She had just won **Female** Movie Star of 2019.

# Zendaya's Life

Zendaya grew up in California.

She has five brothers and sisters.

Both of her parents are very tall!

Q102
All The Hits!
HAVEN
NIGHTCLUB
BOSTON
Zendaya's father
Zendaya's mother

Zendaya always wanted to be an actor.

Her mom worked in a **theater**.

Zendaya was there a lot.

She even acted in some plays.

Then, Zendaya got
jobs in movies.

Her first big part
was in a Spider-Man
movie.

She played a girl
named Michelle.

Zendaya also dances.

She loves **hip-hop** dancing.

When she was 14, she played a dancer on TV!

Zendaya on a TV show

Zendaya was also
on a TV dance show.

Well-known people
teamed up with
dancers.

She won second place!

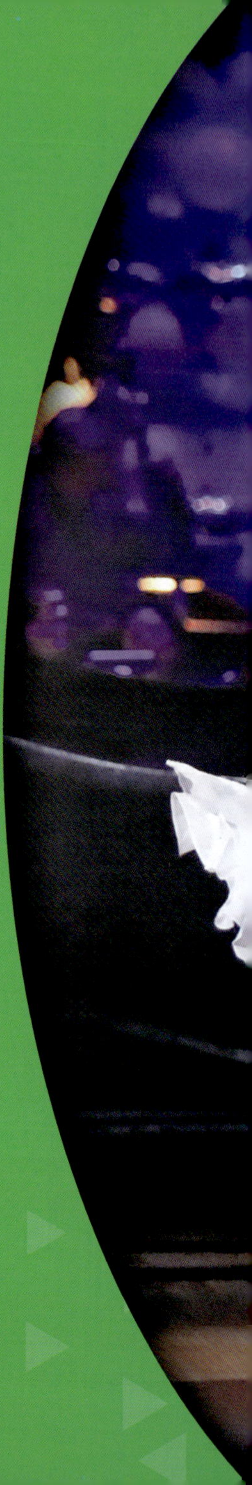

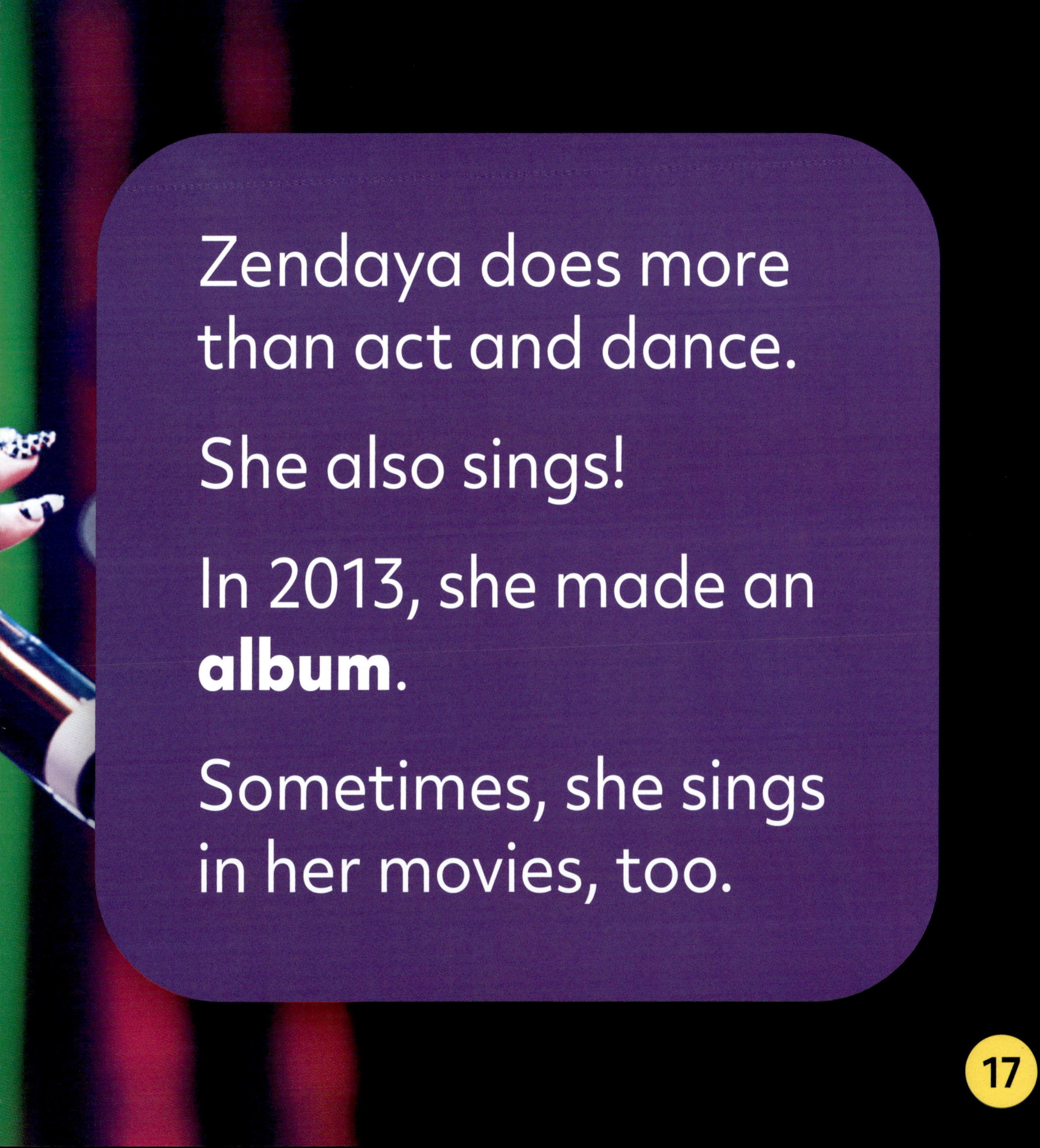

Zendaya does more than act and dance.

She also sings!

In 2013, she made an **album**.

Sometimes, she sings in her movies, too.

Zendaya believes in being kind.

She stands up to bullies.

She wants all kids to believe in themselves.

yoob
one for me.

Zendaya has done many great things.

And she plans to keep going.

What will Zendaya do next?

# Did You Know?

**Born:** September 1, 1996

**Family:** Claire (mother), Kazembe (father), Katianna (sister), Kaylee (sister), AnnaBella (sister), Austin (brother), Julien (brother)

**When she was a kid:** She stopped eating meat.

**Special fact:** Zendaya's name comes from an African language. It means to give thanks.

**Zendaya says:** "You don't have to dance to anyone else's beat except your own."

## Life Connections

Zendaya wants to be herself. She loves who she is. What do you love about yourself?

# Glossary

**album** a group of songs

**female** a girl or a woman

**hip-hop** a style of dance that often goes along with rap music

**theater** a place where movies or plays are shown

# Index

**acting** 8, 17
**California** 6
**dancing** 12, 14, 17, 22
**movies** 4, 11, 17
**singing** 17
**Spider-Man** 11
**TV** 12–14

# Read More

**Bell, Samantha.** *You Can Work in Movies (You Can Work in the Arts).* North Mankato, MN: Capstone (2019).

**Diver, Lucas.** *Zendaya: Disney Channel Actress (Pop Bios).* Minneapolis: Abdo Kids (2015).

# Learn More Online

1. Go to **www.factsurfer.com**
2. Enter "**Zendaya**" into the search box.
3. Click on the cover of this book to see a list of websites.

# About the Author

Rachel Rose writes books for children and teaches yoga. She lives in San Francisco with her husband and her dog, Sandy.